May Your Holidays
Be *Merry*
and *Bright*

ISBN: 978-1-68088-255-1

▉ and Blue Mountain Press are registered in U.S. Patent and Trademark Office. Certain trademarks are used under license.

Printed in China.
First Printing: 2018   ·

✪ This book is printed on recycled paper.

This book is printed on paper that has been specially produced to be acid free (neutral pH) and contains no groundwood or unbleached pulp. It conforms with the requirements of the American National Standards Institute, Inc., so as to ensure that this book will last and be enjoyed by future generations.

Blue Mountain Arts, Inc.
P.O. Box 4549, Boulder, Colorado 80306

May Your Holidays Be *Merry* and *Bright*

Written and Illustrated by
Heather Stillufsen

Blue Mountain Press™
Boulder, Colorado

'Tis the season…
Be *festive*,
be joyful,
and spread some
cheer!

Loved ones
truly make life *merrier,*
so surround yourself
with *friends…*

…and *family.*

Spend time enjoying the
here and now, because
the *present* moment
is a truly
wonderful moment.

Cross a few things off your *winter bucket list:*

- Go ice skating
- Make holiday cookies
- Have a *pajama* day
- Go sledding
- Make snow angels
- *Snuggle* by the fire

Cherish time-honored *traditions* and *memories*…

…and *have fun* creating new ones.

Let your
inner *sparkle* shine,
and know that you are
loved and *appreciated*
by so many.

Recipe for a Happy
Holiday Season:

Mix 1 cup *laughter*
with ¾ cup gratitude.
Add a *positive outlook*,
and mix with lots of love.

Take some time
to *look back* at this year
and think about all you
have made it through and
all you have *achieved*.

Laugh at
your mistakes,
smile at
your *accomplishments*,
and cry at your
goodbyes.

Be *proud* of
all that you are and
all that you have done…
and look forward to
the *future*.

How to make the *most* of a snowy day:

- ♥ Wear a *cozy* sweater
- ♥ Play in the snow
- ♥ Drink *hot cocoa*
- ♥ Spend time with someone you love

Believe in the *magic* of the season, and be *grateful* for all the beautiful *gifts* in your life.

Give *love*…
give time…
give *friendship*
and energy and peace
and forgiveness.
Most of all,
give with all your *heart.*

Remember the *simplest* things are often the *sweetest* things…

…and no winter
is too cold if
you have enough
love.

This holiday season
(and always),
may your days be
merry
and
bright.

About the Author

Heather Stillufsen is an artist and writer who fell in love with drawing as a child and has been holding a pencil ever since. Best known for her delicate and whimsical illustration style, her work is instantly recognizable. From friendship to family to fashion, Heather's

Photo by Christine E. Allen

art demonstrates a contemporary sensibility for people of all ages. Her words are written from the heart and offer those who read them the hope of a brighter day and inspiration to live life to the fullest.

Heather is the author and illustrator of four books: *Sisters Make Life More Beautiful*, *Mothers and Daughters Are Connected by the Heart*, *May Your Holidays Be Merry and Bright*, and *Life Is Tough… but So Are You*.

In addition to her books, Heather's refreshing and elegant illustrations can be found on greeting cards, calendars, journals, planners, art prints, hand-painted needlepoint canvases, and more.

She currently lives in New Jersey with her husband, two daughters, and chocolate Lab.